MIND-BOGGLING
MACHINES
AND
AMAZING MAZES

BY
EDMOND DAVIS

Turner Publishing, Inc.

ATLANTA

Mind-Boggling Machines and Amazing Mazes

Edmond Davis has created twelve fantastic and fascinating challenges to test your wits. Can you follow the mazes and find your way through his fiendish and cunning contraptions?

Each mind-boggling maze asks you to find a correct route or path through the picture. Answers are provided at the back of the book. There you'll also discover more things to look for, either as you solve each puzzle or after you've completed them all. Have fun!

Acknowledgments
Editor: Andrew Farrow
Turner Assistant Editor: Crawford Barnett
Designer: Cathy Tincknell
Puzzle testers: Many people have helped test the mazes.
Particular thanks go to Peter Dickman, Sue Reid,
Jo Hanks, and Jonathan and Samuel Adams.
Production controller: Christine Campbell

CONTENTS

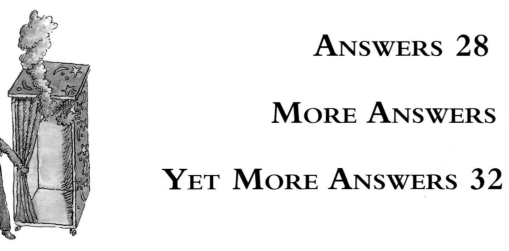

THE STAR FACTORY

Astronauts in this orbiting space factory gather lumps of interstellar rock and transmogrify them into beautiful, shiny stars. Can you find the route the rocks must take so that perfect golden stars are released into the heavens?

LOST IN SPACE?
What other objects has the factory made, and how many astronauts are there in the picture? *Answers on page 28.*

KNIT WITS

Who would imagine it—all this work to knit a stocking cap! But which pathway, for both the sheep and the people, leads to a happy customer?

COUNTING SHEEP

Once you've threaded your way through the machinery, can you find out how many real sheep are in the maze? Don't fall asleep counting them, though... *Answers on page 29.*

PENELOPE'S LAB

Professor Penelope Pinkpotion is seeking fame and fortune. She has developed a fabulous new plant food that will make tomatoes grow fatter and juicier than ever before.

FIND THE FORMULA

Can you unravel the tangle of technical tubing and tentacled technicians to find which part of the apparatus successfully produces Penelope's chemical creation? *Answer on page 29.*

Professor
Penelope

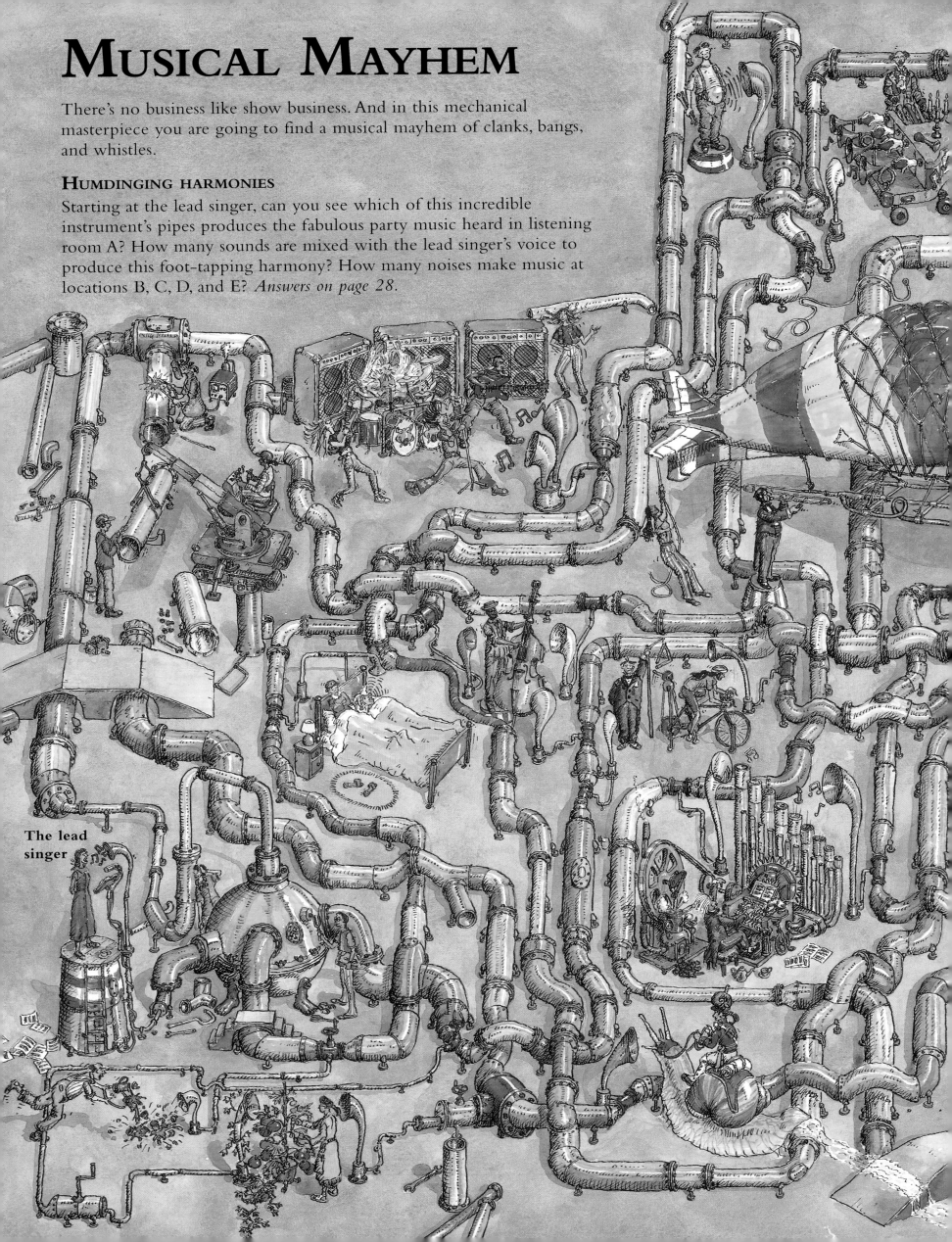

MUSICAL MAYHEM

There's no business like show business. And in this mechanical masterpiece you are going to find a musical mayhem of clanks, bangs, and whistles.

HUMDINGING HARMONIES

Starting at the lead singer, can you see which of this incredible instrument's pipes produces the fabulous party music heard in listening room A? How many sounds are mixed with the lead singer's voice to produce this foot-tapping harmony? How many noises make music at locations B, C, D, and E? *Answers on page 28.*

The lead singer

11

TIME FOR A SNACK?

Sanjay has been hard at work building a new bridge, and now he wants a snack. But he's left his lunch box at the other side of the site! To help him get past some obstacles, he'll need to bring along some important items. Which is the easiest way, taking the fewest items, for Sanjay to reach his food?

HOW MANY WAYS?

Is there more than one route Sanjay can take, if he uses more items? Watch out for the giant octopus and crayfish! Once you've found the best route, count how many of each handy item appear in the picture.
Answers on page 31.

Sanjay

A1 handy
site-crossing
items

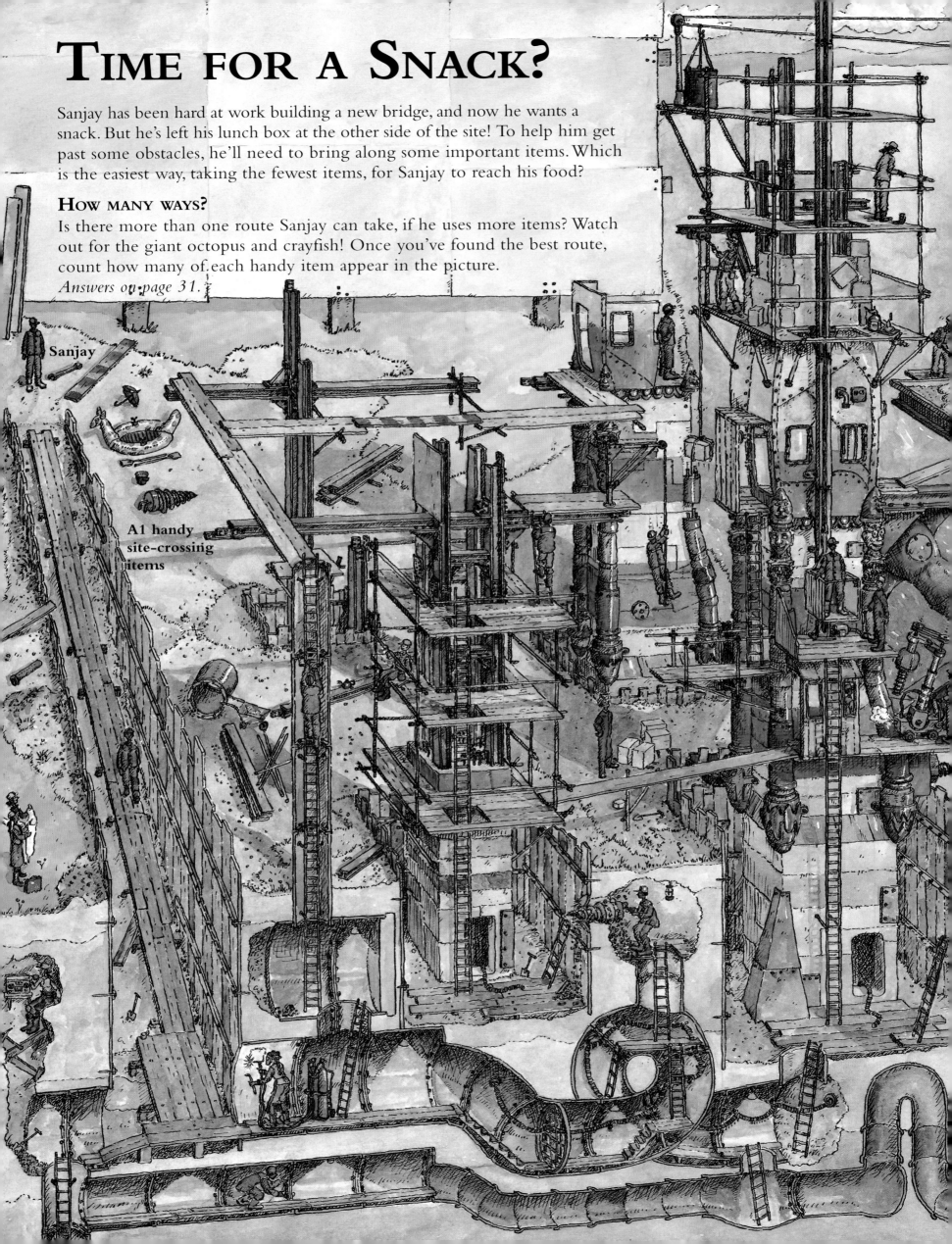

Lunch box

FRUIT CAKES

The chefs in this wacky bakery use a railway to carry their huge mixing bowls. If you had to bake fruit cakes all day long, you might become nutty, too. Can you take railway cars along the right tracks to make their cakes, or will you become derailed?

THE RAILWAY RECIPE

To make your cakes, you must mix a slab of butter, some sugar, a few free-range eggs, flour, milk, and chocolate. Add fruit and nuts, bake gently, then ice and top off with cherries. Have fun, but don't go bananas! *Answer on page 30.*

Start

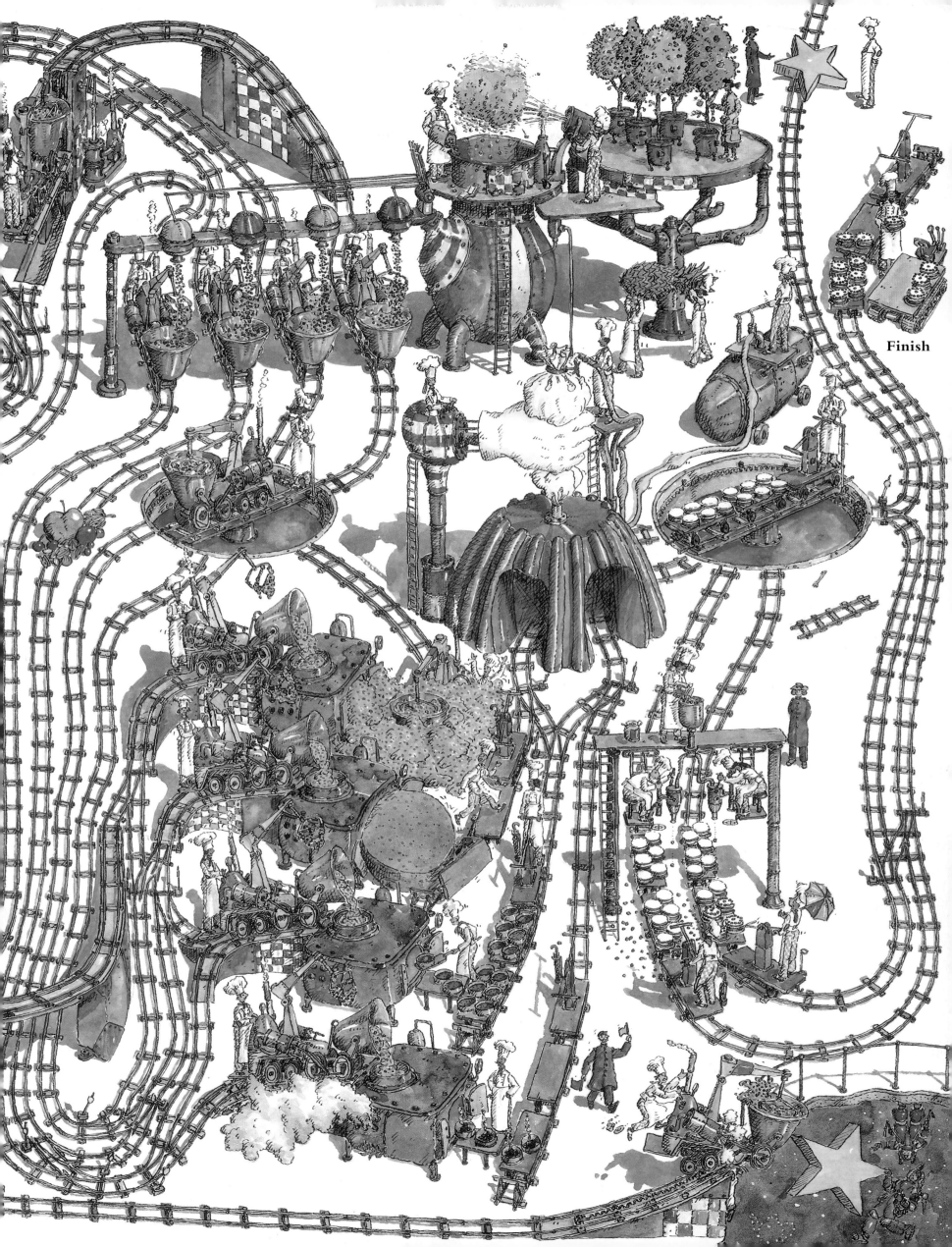

Finish

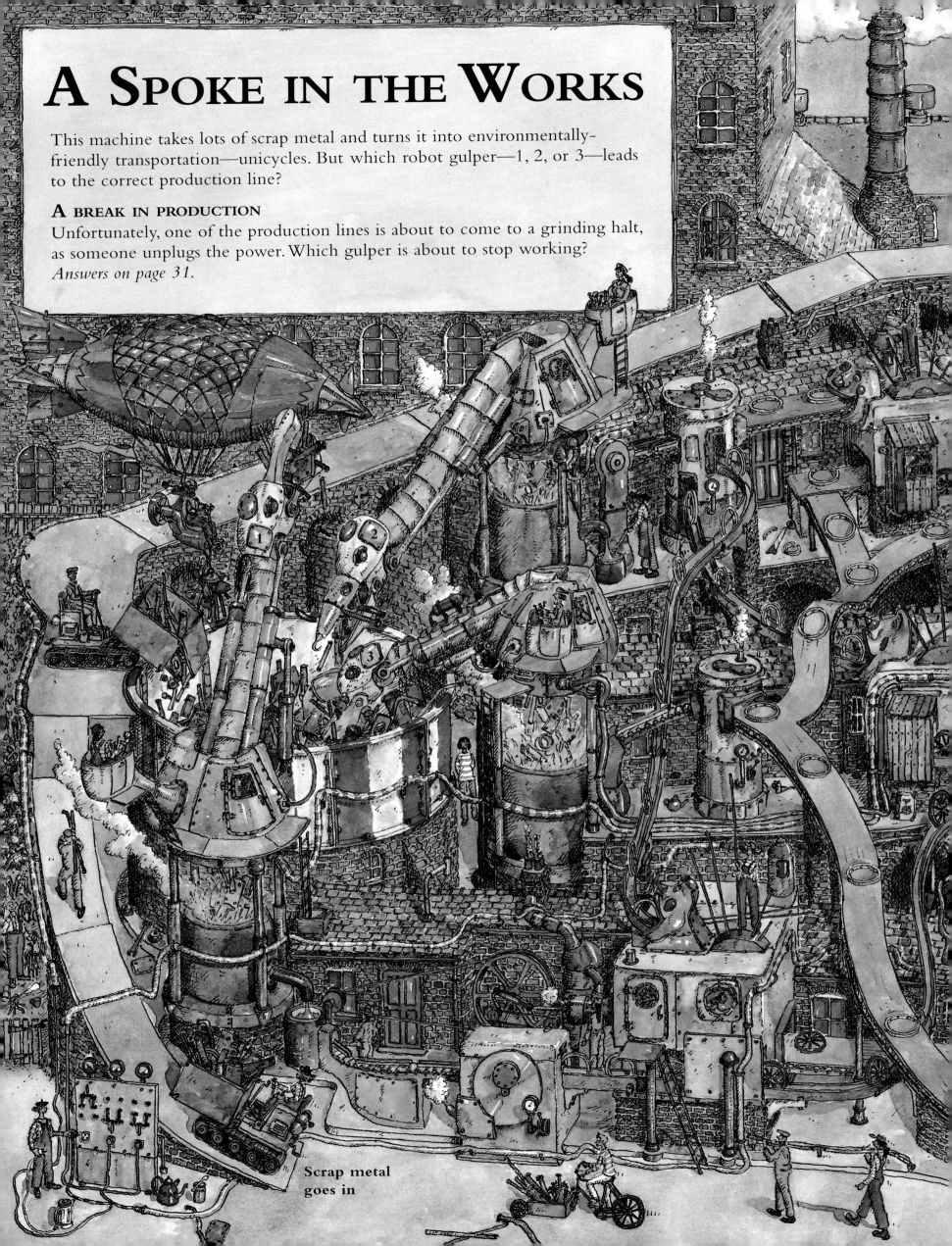

A SPOKE IN THE WORKS

This machine takes lots of scrap metal and turns it into environmentally-friendly transportation—unicycles. But which robot gulper—1, 2, or 3—leads to the correct production line?

A BREAK IN PRODUCTION

Unfortunately, one of the production lines is about to come to a grinding halt, as someone unplugs the power. Which gulper is about to stop working?

Answers on page 31.

Scrap metal
goes in

Perfect
unicycles

A PIECE OF CAKE?

If you desire a nice slice of fruitcake, why not visit The Trick Cyclists' Café? There's never a dull moment in this entertaining establishment, where the service is a trifle unusual—just watch your waiter whiz through the maze!

TRICK CYCLISTS

Can you find the path the waiters must take to reach your table? Don't get it wrong, or your cake might be lost in this fiendish optical illusion. *Answer on page 28.*

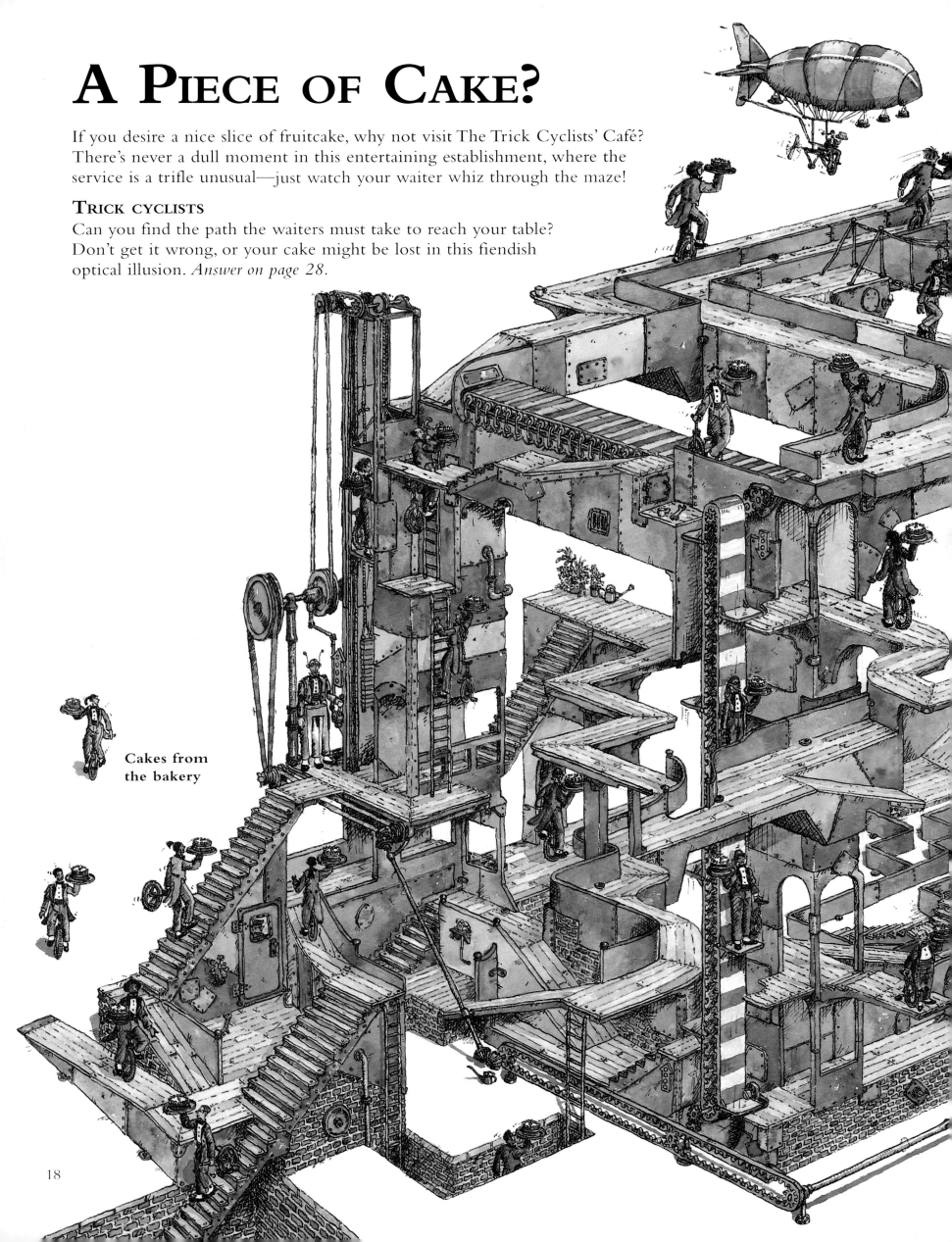

Cakes from the bakery

Satisfied
customers

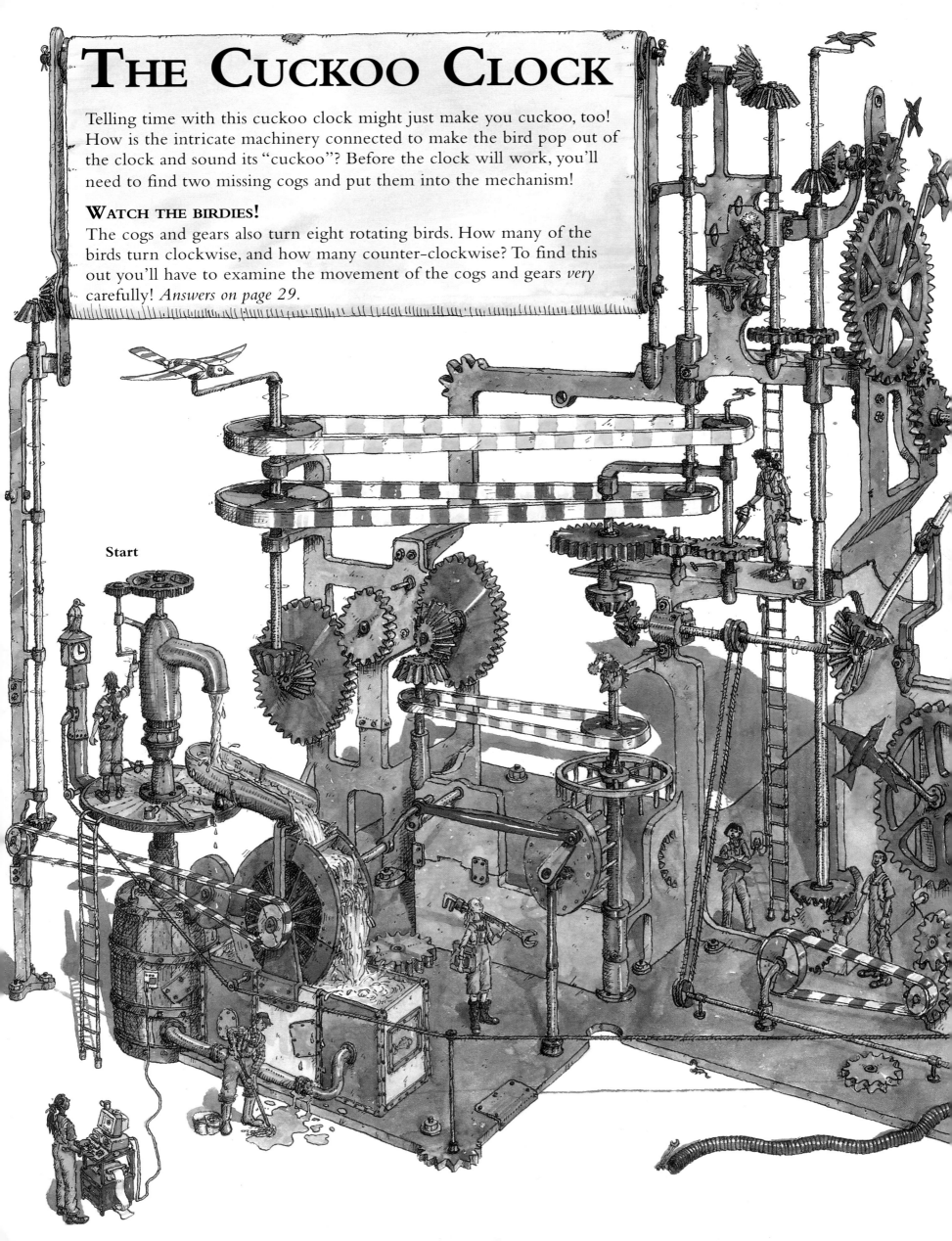

THE CUCKOO CLOCK

Telling time with this cuckoo clock might just make you cuckoo, too! How is the intricate machinery connected to make the bird pop out of the clock and sound its "cuckoo"? Before the clock will work, you'll need to find two missing cogs and put them into the mechanism!

WATCH THE BIRDIES!

The cogs and gears also turn eight rotating birds. How many of the birds turn clockwise, and how many counter-clockwise? To find this out you'll have to examine the movement of the cogs and gears *very* carefully! *Answers on page 29.*

Start

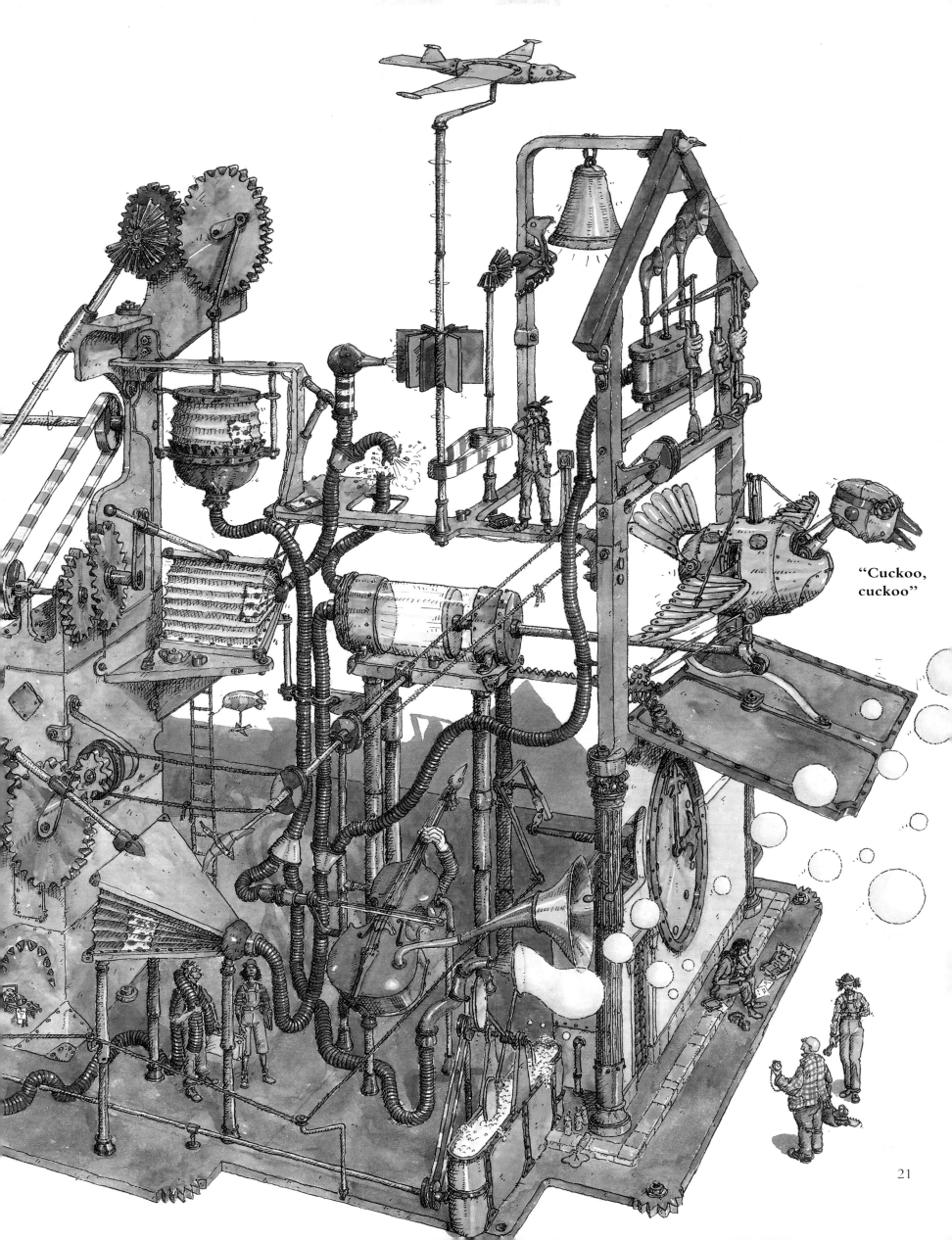

"Cuckoo, cuckoo"

21

CLOWNING AROUND

Barnaby the Clown wants to make the little girl happy by giving her a lollipop. How many ways are there for Barnaby to reach one of the three lollipops hanging in the circus arena and get it to the little girl?

MERRY MAYHEM

Barnaby will need some special gadgets to help him on his way. Can he get through the mayhem with only two items? *Answers on page 31.*

Barnaby

Acme guaranteed circus gadgets

The little girl

WHICH LEVER?

Here's a tricky maze of machinery. Thirsty Thora at table A is gasping for a cup of coffee. Which lever should you pull to give her a drink?

YOU'LL NEED SOME CLUES...

The numbered levers will start machines that boil water *and* make coffee pots. Can you follow the pots as they whiz along the line and find the correct route to Thora? The correct machine must also pipe boiling hot coffee to the table. Have fun, and don't get lost! *Answer on page 30.*

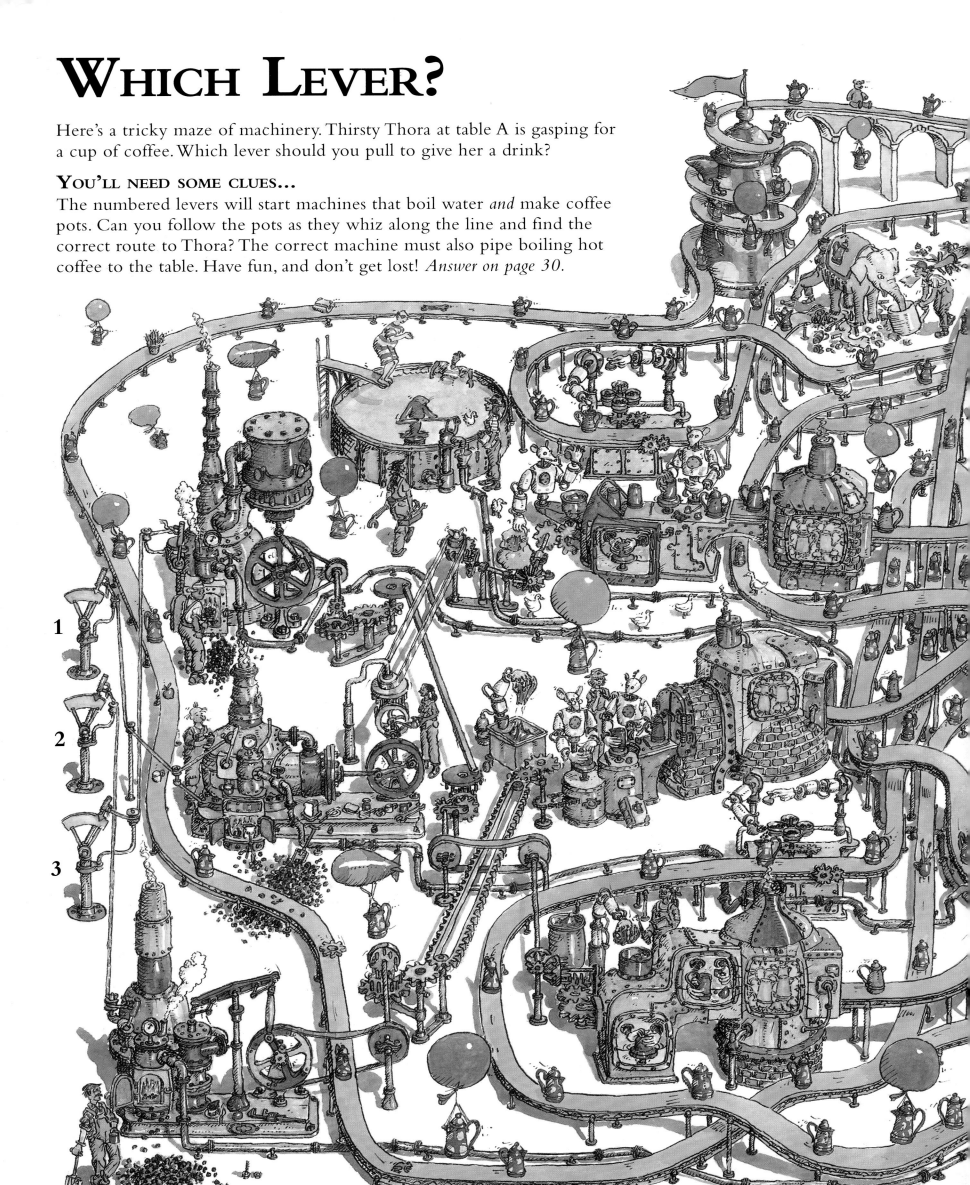

1

2

3

A CLOSE SHAVE!

This looks like havoc at the hairdresser's—everyone is getting ready for a celebration ball. But which way should they steer their cars to get each of the weird and wonderful hairstyles that are offered?

SPOT THE CUSTOMER
Now that you've reached this last maze, you should be able to see that most of the customers come from other *Mind-Boggling Machines and Amazing Mazes* mazes. Which characters are complete strangers? *Answers on page 30.*

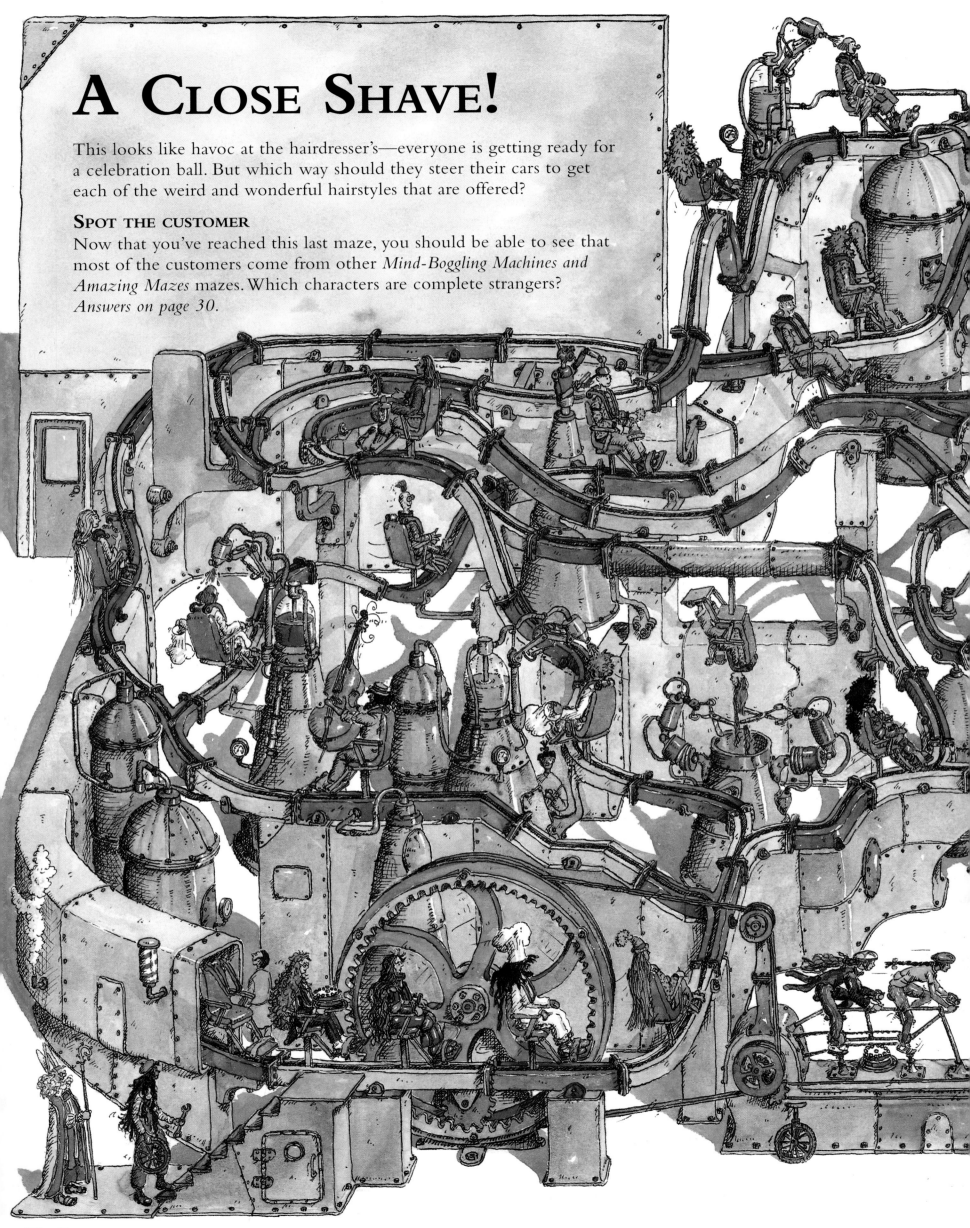

The line

Spiky
blue
cut

Green with
bows

Shiny
purple

Sensible
cut and
wash

Wild
green
curls

27

ANSWERS

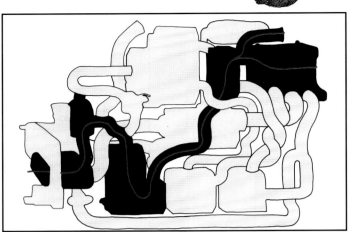

The Star Factory

The correct route is shown on the right. If the wrong route is followed, the factory also makes armchairs and funny faces. Have you found the seventy-four astronauts in the scene?

There are also astronauts in two of the other mazes—can you find them? And in which other maze is there a comfortable armchair? *Answers on page 32.*

A Piece of Cake?

The correct route to the customers is shown below. How did you do? Next, can you find fifty-five black-suited waiters in the scene? And in which other mazes are people cycling? *Answers on page 32.*

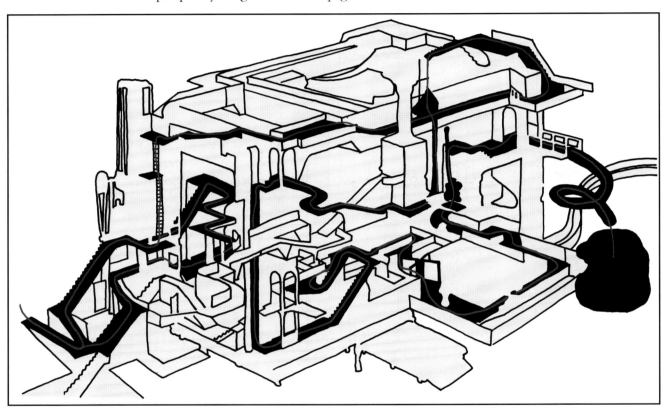

Musical Mayhem

The correct route is shown on the right. Eight sounds are added on the way to room A.

Eleven sounds are added to the trumpet at B—producing quite a blast! There are also eleven sounds added on the way to D, and five on the way to C. The people in room E, who are straining to hear some music, will be disappointed—there's a break in the tubing. When it's repaired, do you think they'll be able to hear anything?

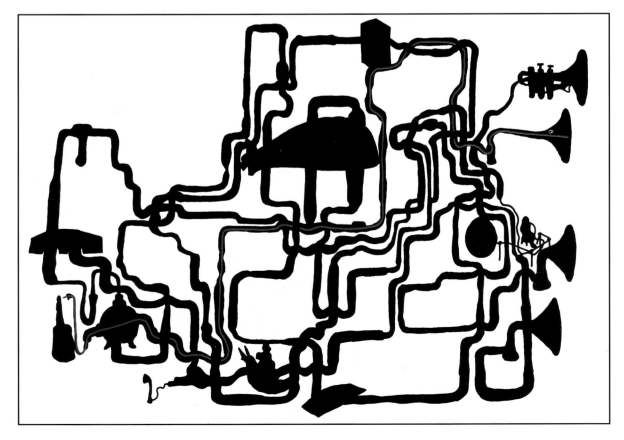

Penelope's Lab

The correct path through the laboratory equipment is shown on the right.

How many test tubes are there in the laboratory equipment? There are also two robot octopuses making the plant food—can you find the two *real* octopuses hidden somewhere in the other mazes?

Answers on page 32.

Knit Wits

Route 1 will produce a normal cap. The correct route is shown on the left. There are sixty-three real sheep in the maze.

Can you find four other tiny sheep in the picture? Can you find a sheep in one of the other mazes? And can you spot a visitor from another maze? *Answers on page 32.*

The Cuckoo Clock

The correct routes to the cuckoo bird are shown on the right. The positions of the missing cogs are shown by red circles. The rotating bird shown by the blue circle turns clockwise—the other seven turn counter-clockwise.

Now, in which of the other mazes is there another cuckoo clock? *Answer on page 32.*

MORE ANSWERS

A Close Shave!

The correct routes are shown on the right. The caveman and the bishop are complete strangers in the maze. (Did you think it was the alien? It has come from the Star Factory.)

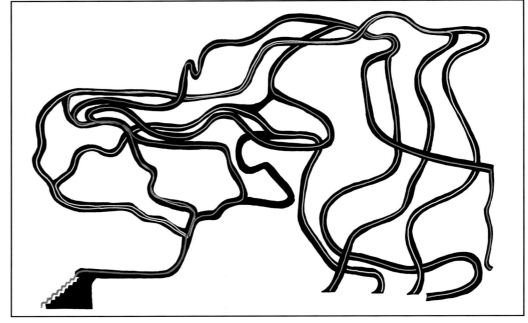

Fruit Cakes

Have you been able to follow this difficult maze? The correct route is shown on the left. If you took the wrong route, did you not notice that some of the dispensers do not work properly?

Which Lever?

You should pull lever 2. The correct routes are shown on the right. Did you see that lever 3 will deliver a pot to table C, but that it only sends hot coffee to tables B and D? Did you discover that table C gets cold water from the swimming pool, and that odd ingredients are added on some of the routes?

Can you find some flowers, an old boot, and a cuddly toy on the conveyors? How many balloons and zeppelins are there in the picture? How many complete coffee pots are on the green conveyors? And which person is obviously a visitor from another maze?
Answers on page 32.

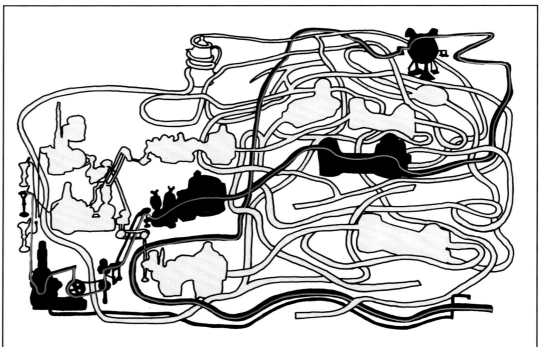

Time for a Snack?

Sanjay needs to take the drill, the plank, and the wrench to get to his lunch box. The correct route is shown in red, on the right. He can also follow the blue route, but that's a much longer way around. There's no other way for him to go, even if he takes more items. As for the tools Sanjay has to choose from, there are two drills, five planks, four wrenches, seven inflatable boats and an umbrella.

Can you count how many wrenches there are in all twelve mazes? *Answer on page 32.*

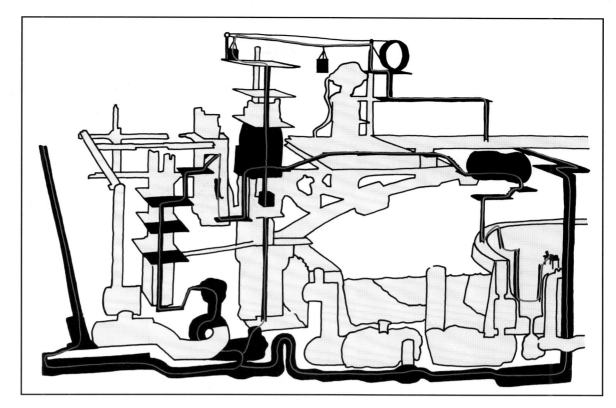

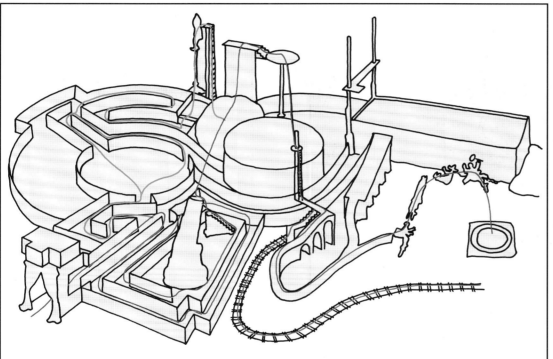

Clowning Around

Barnaby must take three items. The easiest way for Barnaby is shown in red on the left—he needs to take the climbing suckers, an umbrella, and the spring-heeled boots. The blue route shows another way, but Barnaby will have to take four items—the climbing suckers, an umbrella, a key for the clockwork camel, and a bucket of water. Barnaby could also follow the green routes, but he'd need at least five items, including a bucket of water and a chair to get past the ferocious lion and tigers!

In the circus, clowns disappear from the magician's booth—can you find out in which other mazes they reappear? *Answer on page 32.*

A Spoke in the Works

Robot gulper 2 leads along the right production line. The correct line is shown in red on the right. Gulper 1's power line (shown in blue) is about to be turned off.

All of the wheels on the factory's production lines have ten spokes— except for one. Can you find it? *Answer on page 32.*

YET MORE ANSWERS

THE STAR FACTORY
The astronauts appear in a hole in the space-time fabric of the Fruit Cakes bakery, and in A Close Shave. There's a comfy armchair in A Piece of Cake.

KNIT WITS
There's also a sheep in A Close Shave. The musician with the cello is a visitor from Musical Mayhem.

PENELOPE'S LAB
There are twenty-four test tubes in the picture—did you count the ones that are being spun by the mechanical octopuses? There's a giant octopus in Time for a Snack and a small one in Which Lever.

MUSICAL MAYHEM
Do you think they'll hear the tomatoes growing, the moving snail, and the pin drop?

TIME FOR A SNACK?
There are at least fifty-six wrenches in the maze.

A SPOKE IN THE WORKS
There's a wheel with eleven spokes. It is the one being squashed into a square.

A PIECE OF CAKE?
There are cyclists in Time for a Snack, Musical Mayhem, A Spoke in the Works, A Close Shave, and Clowning Around.

THE CUCKOO CLOCK
There's another cuckoo clock in A Spoke in the Works.

CLOWNING AROUND
The clowns have appeared in Musical Mayhem, Time for a Snack, Fruit Cakes, and A Close Shave.

WHICH LEVER?
There are thirty-seven balloons and zeppelins, and 207 complete coffee pots on the conveyors. The violinist is the visitor.

AND THERE'S MORE!

Can you find sixteen zeppelins in the mazes?
In which two scenes could you make a telephone call?
Can you find a photograph of a clown?
Can you find 125 real animals, including two white rabbits, three mice, and four tiny snails, in the puzzles?

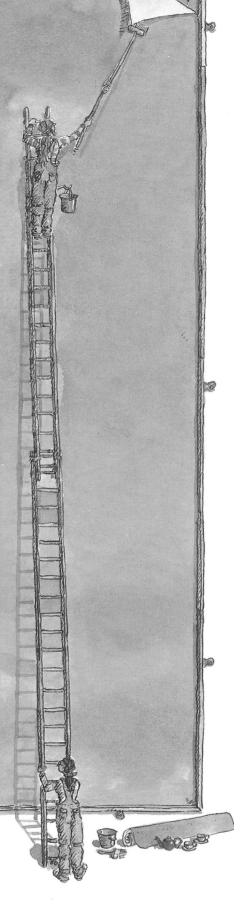

First Published in Great Britain in 1995 by
Hamlyn Children's Books,
an imprint of Reed Children's Books,
Michelin House, 81 Fulham Road, London SW3 6RB,
and in Auckland, Melbourne, Singapore, and Toronto.

Illustrations copyright © 1995 Edmond Davis
Text copyright © 1995 Reed International Books Limited

First Published in the U.S.A. by
Turner Publishing, Inc.
A Subsidiary of Turner Broadcasting System, Inc.
1050 Techwood Drive, N.W.
Atlanta, Georgia 30318

Library of Congress
Cataloging-in-Publication Data

Davis, Edmond, 1960–
    Mind-boggling machines and amazing mazes / Edmond Davis.
        p.   cm.
    Summary: Maze puzzles challenge readers to find their way through such places as a large factory, wacky bakery, and circus bigtop.
    ISBN 1-57036-201-7   (a1k. paper)
    1. Machinery—Juvenile literature.   2. Maze puzzles—Juvenile literature.   [1. Maze puzzles.   2. Puzzles.]   I. Title
TJ147.D38   1995
793.73—dc20   95–16798
                                                                CIP
                                                                AC

First Edition   10 9 8 7 6 5 4 3 2 1

Printed in Italy